Man's Best Friend

HARVEST HOUSE PUBLISHERS

EUGENE, OREGON

Artwork by John Weiss

Artwork designs are reproduced under license © 2007 by The Greenwich Workshop, Inc., and may not be reproduced without permission. For more information regarding the artwork in this book, please contact:

> The Greenwich Workshop
> PO Box 231
> Seymour, CT 06483
> (800) 243-4246
> www.greenwichworkshop.com

Design and production by Koechel Peterson & Associates, Inc., Minneapolis, Minnesota

Harvest House Publishers has made every effort to trace the ownership of all poems and quotes. In the event of a question arising from the use of a poem or quote, we regret any error made and will be pleased to make the necessary correction in future editions of this book.

MAN'S BEST FRIEND

Text copyright © 2007 by Harvest House Publishers
Published by Harvest House Publishers
Eugene, Oregon 97402

ISBN-13: 978-0-7369-1849-7
ISBN-10: 0-7369-1849-3

Printed in China

07 08 09 10 11 12 13 14 / LP / 10 9 8 7 6 5 4 3 2 1

Recollect that the Almighty, who gave the dog to be companion of our pleasures and our toils, hath invested him with a nature noble and incapable of deceit.

Sir Walter Scott
THE TALISMAN

The great pleasure of a dog is that you may make a fool of yourself with him and not only will he not scold you, but he will make a fool of himself too.

Samuel Butler

Tribute to a Dog

The one absolutely unselfish friend that man can have in this selfish world, the one that never deserts him, the one that never proves ungrateful or treacherous, is his dog.

A man's dog stands by him in prosperity and in poverty. In health and in sickness. He will sleep on the cold ground, where the wintry winds blow and the snow drives fiercely, if only he may be near his master's side. He will kiss the hand that has no food to offer; he will lick the wounds and sores that come in encounters with the roughness of the world.

He guards the sleep of his pauper master as if he were a prince. When all other friends desert, he remains. When riches take wing and reputation falls to pieces, he is as constant in his love as the sun in its journey through the heavens.

Senator George Vest

'Tis sweet to hear the watch-dog's honest bark
Bay deep-mouthed welcome as we draw near home;
'Tis sweet to know there is an eye will mark
Our coming, and look brighter when we come.

Lord Byron

They are better than human beings
because they know but do not tell.

Emily Dickinson

We never really own a dog
as much as he owns us.

Gene Hill

You are my friend and I hope you know that's true.
No matter what happens, I will stand by you.
I'll be there for you whenever you need,
To lend you a hand, to do a good deed.
So just call on me when you need me, my friend.
I will always be there, even to the end.

Author unknown

I talk to him when I'm lonesome like,
 and I'm sure he understands.
When he looks at me so attentively,
 and gently licks my hands;
Then he rubs his nose on my tailored clothes,
 but I never say naught thereat,
For the good Lord knows I can buy more clothes,
 but never a friend like that!

W. Dayton Wedgefarth

Kindness is more than deeds.
It is an attitude, an expression,
a look, a touch. It is anything
that lifts another person.

C. Neil Strait

Friendship is
warmth in cold,
firm ground in a bog.

Miles Franklin

O the world is wide and the world is grand,
And there's little or nothing new,
But its sweetest thing is the grip of the hand
Of the friend who's tried and true.

Author unknown

Working there…guarding our precious bread corn from the varmints,
I came to see what I would have been up against if I'd had it to do
without the help of Old Yeller.…Also, look at all the fun I would have
missed if I'd been alone, and how lonesome I would have been. I had to
admit Papa had been right when he'd told me how bad I needed a dog.

Fred Gipson
OLD YELLER

Thus nature has no love for solitude, and
always leans, as it were, on some support;
and the sweetest support is found in the
most intimate friendship.

Cicero

He cannot be a gentleman which
loveth not a dog.

John North Brooke

The greatest healing therapy
is friendship and love.

Hubert Humphrey

A dog is the only thing on this
earth that loves you more
than he loves himself.

Josh Billings

The dog represents all
that is best in man.

Etienne Charlet

Working with the dogs every day helps me with my frustrations.
I learn how to deal with my problems better and communicate
with people like I communicate with the dogs.

Angel, an at-risk teen

A friend is there when everyone else isn't, believing when
everyone else hasn't, understanding when everyone else
doesn't, and loving when everyone else wasn't.

Author unknown

There are times when only a dog will do for a friend.... When
you're beaten sick and blue, and the world's all wrong, for he won't
care if you break and cry, or grouch...for he'll let you know as he
licks your hand that he's downright sorry...and understands.

Don Blanding

We give them the love we can spare, the time we can
spare. In return dogs have given us their absolute all.
It is without doubt the best deal man has ever made.

Roger Caras

My Dog's My Boss

Each day when it's anighing three
  Old Dick looks at the clock,
Then proudly brings my stick to me
  To mind me of our walk.
And in his doggy rapture he
  Does everything but talk.

But since I lack his zip and zest
  My old bones often tire;
And so I ventured to suggest
  Today we hug the fire.
But with what wailing he expressed
  The death of his desire!

He gazed at me with eyes of woe
  As if to say: "Old Boy,
You mustn't lose your grip, you know,
  Let us with laughing joy,
On heath and hill six miles or so
  Our legs and lungs employ,"

And then his bark stilled to a sigh
  He flopped upon the floor;
But such a soft old mug am I
  I threw aside the door;
So gaily, though the wind was high
  We hiked across the moor.

Robert Service

Properly trained, a man
can be dog's best friend.
Corey Ford

If you can't decide
between a Shepherd,
a Setter, or a Poodle,
get them all...adopt
a mutt!
ASPCA

Until one has loved an animal, a part of one's soul remains unawakened.

Anatole France

"Dogs, sir?"

"Not just now," said Mr. Winkle.

"Ah! You should keep dogs—fine animals—sagacious creatures—dog of my own once—pointer—surprising instinct—out shooting one day—entering enclosure—whistled—dog stopped—whistled again—Ponto—no go; stock still—called —Ponto, Ponto—wouldn't move—dog transfixed—staring at a board—looked up, saw an inscription— 'Gamekeeper has orders to shoot all dogs found in this enclosure.' —wouldn't pass it—wonderful dog—valuable dog that—very."

"Singular circumstance that," said Mr. Pickwick. "Will you allow me to make a note of it?"

"Certainly, sir, certainly—hundred more anecdotes of the same animal."

Charles Dickens
PICKWICK PAPERS

The dog is man's best friend.
He has a tail on one end.
Up in front he has teeth.
And four legs underneath.

Ogden Nash

Charley likes to get up early, and he likes me to get up early too. And why shouldn't he? Right after his breakfast he goes back to sleep. Over the years he has developed a number of innocent-appearing ways to get me up. He can shake himself and his collar loud enough to wake the dead. If that doesn't work he gets a sneezing fit. But perhaps his most irritating method is to sit quietly beside the bed and stare into my face with a sweet and forgiving look on his face; I come out of deep sleep with the feeling of being looked at. But I have learned to keep my eyes tight shut. If I even blink he sneezes and stretches, and the night's sleep is over for me. Often the war of wills goes on for quite a time, I squinching my eyes shut and he forgiving me, but he nearly always wins. He liked travelling so much he wanted to get started early, and early for Charley is the first tempering of darkness with the dawn.

John Steinbeck
TRAVELS WITH CHARLEY

If a dog will not come to you after having looked you in the face, you should go home and examine your conscience.

Woodrow Wilson

Friendship is unnecessary, like philosophy, like art....It has no survival value; rather it is one of those things that give value to survival.

C.S. Lewis

Acquiring a dog may be the only opportunity
a human ever has to choose a relative.

Mordecai Siegal

[The puppy's] the only one who has taught me that whatever adversity there is, you can conquer it.

Officer Carr

Dogs are not our whole life, but they make our lives whole.

Roger Caras

No one appreciates the very special genius of your conversation as the dog does.

Christopher Morley

To look at Montmorency you would imagine that he was an angel sent upon earth, for some reason withheld from mankind, in the shape of a small fox-terrier. There is a sort of Oh-what-a-wicked-world-this-is-and-how-I-wish-I-could-do-something-to-make-it-better-and-nobler expression about Montmorency that has been known to bring tears into the eyes of pious ladies and gentlemen.

When first he came to live at my expense, I never thought I should be able to get him to stop long. I used to sit down and look at him, as he sat on the rug and looked up at me, and think: "Oh, that dog will never live. He will be snatched up to the bright skies in a chariot, that is what will happen to him."

But when I had paid for about a dozen chickens that he had killed; and had dragged him, growling and kicking, by the scruff of his neck, out of a hundred and fourteen street fights; and had had a dead cat brought round for my inspection by an irate female, who called me a murderer; and had been summoned by the man next door but one for having a ferocious dog at large, that had kept him penned up in his own tool-shed, afraid to venture his nose outside the door for over two hours on a cold night; and had learned that the gardener, unknown to myself, had won thirty shillings by backing him to kill rats against time, then I began to think that maybe they'd let him remain on earth for a bit longer, after all.

To hang about a stable, and collect a gang of the most disreputable dogs to be found in the room, and lead them out to march round the shims to fight other disreputable dogs, is Montmorency's idea of "life": and so, as I before observed, he gave to the suggestion of inns, and pubs, and hotels his most emphatic approbation.

Jerome K. Jerome
THREE MEN IN A BOAT

How many of us go through our days parched and empty, thirsting after happiness, when we're really standing knee-deep in the river of abundance?

Sarah Ban Breathnach

A dog hath true love,
A dog hath right good understanding,
A wise dog knoweth all things,
A dog hath force and kindliness,
A dog hath mettle and is comely,
A dog is in all things seemly.
A knowing dog thinketh no evil,
A dog hath a memory that forgeteth not,
I say unto you again a dog forsaketh not his duty,
Hath might and cunning therewith and a great brave heart.

Gace de la Vigne

A dog is not "almost human," and I know of no greater insult to the canine race than to describe it as such.

John Holmes

You are to know then, that as it is likeness that begets affection, so my favourite dog is a little one, a lean one, and none of the finest shaped. He is not much spaniel in his fawning, but has (what might be worth any man's while to imitate him in) a dumb, surly sort of kindness that rather shows itself when he thinks me ill-used by others, than when we walk quietly or peaceably by ourselves. If it be the chief point of friendship to comply with a friend's motions and inclinations, he possesses this in an eminent degree: he lies down when I sit, and walks when I walk, which is more than many good friends can pretend to.

Alexander Pope

There's facts about dogs, and then there's opinions about them. The dogs have the facts, and the humans have the opinions. If you want the facts about the dog, always get them straight from the dog. If you want opinions, get them from humans.

J. Allen Boone

The fidelity of a dog is a precious gift demanding no less binding moral responsibilities than the friendship of a human being. The bond with a dog is as lasting as the ties of this earth can ever be.

Konrad Lorenz

The next time you get angry at someone or start thinking of I, ME, MY, and MINE instead of what you can do for others, take a few lessons in life from man's best friend, the dog, and this country and the world would be a better place to live.

Pearce W. Hammond

A dog is like an eternal Peter Pan, a child who never grows old and who therefore is always available to love and be loved.

Aaron Katcher

No man can be condemned for owning a dog. As long as he has a dog,
he has a friend; and the poorer he gets, the better friend he has.

Will Rogers

I think dogs are the most amazing creatures; they give unconditional love.
For me they are the role model for being alive.

Gilda Radner